FAST CARS

LAMBORGHINI

by Randal C. Hill

Reading Consultant:
Barbara J. Fox
Reading Specialist
North Carolina State University

Content Consultant:
James Elliott
Editor
Classic & Sports Car magazine

Capstone

Mankato, Minnesota

Blazers is published by Capstone Press,
151 Good Counsel Drive, P.O. Box 669, Mankato, Minnesota 56002.
www.capstonepress.com

Library of Congress Cataloging-in-Publication Data
Hill, Randal C.
   Lamborghini / by Randal C. Hill.
   p. cm.—(Blazers. Fast cars)
   Includes bibliographical references and index.
   ISBN-13: 978-1-4296-0102-3 (hardcover)
   ISBN-10: 1-4296-0102-7 (hardcover)
   1. Lamborghini automobile—Juvenile literature. I. Title. II. Series.
TL215.L33H55 2008
629.222—dc22   2007004905

Summary: Simple text and colorful photographs describe the history and models
   of the Lamborghini.

Essential content terms are **bold** and are defined at the bottom of the page
where they first appear.

Editorial Credits
Mandy Robbins, editor; Bobbi J. Wyss, designer; Jo Miller, photo researcher

Photo Credits
Alamy/Alvey & Towers Picture Library, 10–11; Transtock Inc./Martyn Goddard,
   14–15
AP/Wide World Photos/Keystone/Martial Trezzini, 25
Corbis/Car Culture, 13 (top), 16–17
Rex USA/Stewart Cook, 22–23
Ron Kimball Stock/Chia Wen, 28–29; Ron Kimball, 4–5, 6–7, 12, 13 (bottom),
   20–21, 24, 26–27
Shutterstock/Alexey Zarubin, cover
VL Communications, 8–9
ZUMA Press/Michael Tweed, 18–19

1 2 3 4 5 6 12 11 10 09 08 07

TABLE OF CONTENTS

The Road Rocket 4

The Need for Speed. 9

Current Models 14

Special Features 22

Living Legend 26

Timeline 12

Diagram 20

Glossary 30

Read More 31

Internet Sites 31

Index 32

chapter 1

THE ROAD ROCKET

A Lamborghini's engine revs as it whips along a country road. Like the charging bull on the hood ornament, its power is easy to see.

The driver presses the pedal to the floor. The car leaps forward with a loud roar. In a flash, the shiny sports car thunders down the road.

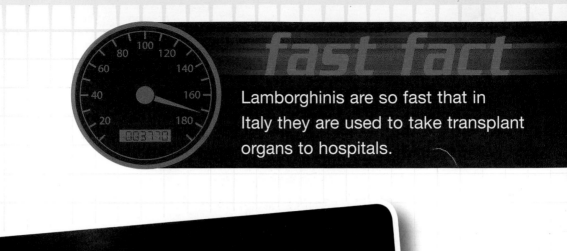

Lamborghinis are so fast that in Italy they are used to take transplant organs to hospitals.

Ferruccio Lamborghini

chapter 2

THE NEED FOR SPEED

Ferruccio Lamborghini grew up in a small Italian village. He worked on engines during World War II. After the war, he started building tractors.

Though his business was tractors, Lamborghini's real love was sports cars. By the early 1960s, he had earned enough money to buy a Ferrari.

Lamborghini tractor

LAMBORGHINI TIMELINE

When Lamborghini's Ferrari had problems, he took it to the manufacturer. But instead of fixing the problem, the company's owner was rude to him.

The first Lamborghini, the 350 GT, is sold.

1964

The Espada is released.

1968

1966

The Miura is introduced.

Fed up with Ferrari, Lamborghini decided to build the finest sports cars in the world. His first production car, the 350 GT, went on sale in 1964.

The V10 Gallardo is released.

2003

1972

1990

2002

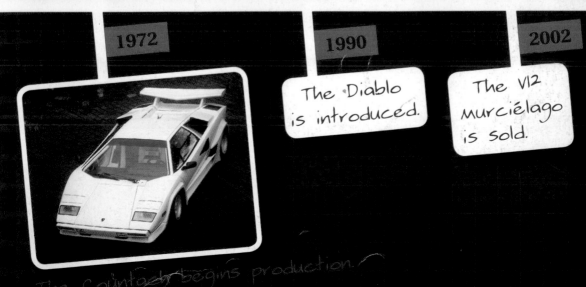

The Diablo is introduced.

The V12 Murciélago is sold.

The Countach begins production.

chapter 3

CURRENT MODELS

Every Lamborghini is built with **_all-wheel drive_**. The cars also have special racing tires, brakes, and suspension systems.

all-wheel drive — a system where power is sent from the drive shaft to all four wheels.

2005 Lamborghini Gallardo

The V10 Gallardo is Lamborghini's entry–level model. This car springs from 0 to 62 miles (100 km) per hour in just 4.2 seconds.

2007 Lamborghini Murciélago LP640 Roadster

In 2002, the V12 Murciélago amazed the world with its style and speed. **Ceramic** brakes were added in 2006. They react more quickly than other brakes for better control.

ceramic — describes a system of clay brakes that work better than standard brakes

MURCIÉLAGO DIAGRAM

door mirror

high-intensity headlamp

air intake

engine

alloy wheel

21

chapter 4

SPECIAL FEATURES

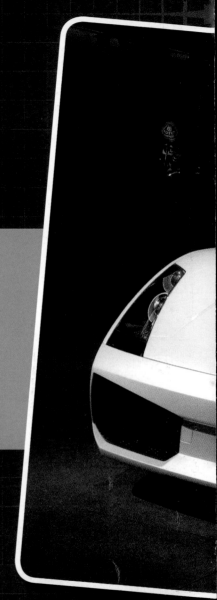

Each Lamborghini model has features that set it apart. The Gallardo Spyder has a folding top that is stored behind the engine area.

The Murciélago LP640 has a glass engine cover to show off its powerful motor. The Murciélago Roadster is nearly twice as wide as it is tall.

2006 Lamborghini Murciélago Roadster

fast fact

Lamborghini is often called the House of the Bull. Most Lamborghinis are named after famous Spanish fighting bulls.

chapter 5

LIVING LEGEND

The newest Lamborghini **concept car** is a new take on the 1960s Miura. The design will have a 700-horsepower engine.

concept car —
a vehicle built to show off an idea

1967 Lamborghini Miura

2006 Miura concept car

The future of Lamborghini is sure to be fast and exciting. Sports car lovers can expect bold moves from the House of the Bull.

fast fact

Buyers must wait up to two years for their Lamborghinis.

GLOSSARY

all-wheel drive (AHL-WEEL DRIVE)—a drive system where power is sent from the drive shaft to all four wheels

ceramic (suh-RAM-ik)—having to do with objects made out of clay

concept car (KON-sept KAR)—a vehicle built to show off an idea

feature (FEE-chuhr)—an important part or quality of something

horsepower (HORSS-pou-ur)—a unit for measuring an engine's power

manufacturer (man-yuh-FAK-chur-ur)—a person or company that makes a product

production car (pruh-DUHK-shuhn KAHR)—a vehicle produced for mass-market sale

suspension (suh-SPEN-shuhn)—the system of springs and shock absorbers that cushions a car's up-and-down movements

READ MORE

Doeden, Matt. *Sports Cars.* Horsepower. Mankato, Minn.: Capstone Press, 2005.

Graham, Ian. *Sports Cars.* Designed for Success. Chicago: Heinemann, 2003.

McKenna, A. T. *Lamborghini.* Ultimate Cars. Edina, Minn.: Abdo, 2002.

INTERNET SITES

FactHound offers a safe, fun way to find Internet sites related to this book. All of the sites on FactHound have been researched by our staff.

Here's how:
1. Visit *www.facthound.com*
2. Choose your grade level.
3. Type in this special code **1429601027** for age-appropriate sites. You may also browse subjects by clicking on letters, or by clicking on pictures or words.
4. Click on the **Fetch It** button.

FactHound will fetch the best sites for you!

INDEX

all-wheel drive, 14

brakes, 14, 19

concept cars, 26

drivers, 6

engines, 4, 9, 22, 24, 26

Ferraris, 10, 12

history, 9–10, 12–13
hood ornaments, 4
House of the Bull, 25, 29

Lamborghini, Ferruccio, 9–10, 12–13

models
350 GT, 12, 13
Countach, 13
Diablo, 13
Espada, 12
Gallardo, 17
Gallardo Spyder, 22
Miura, 12, 26
Murciélago, 13, 19
Murciélago LP640, 24
Murciélago Roadster, 24

production cars, 13

speed, 7, 17
suspension systems, 14

tires, 14
tractors, 9, 10

World War II, 9